The Great Swamp
New Jersey's Natural Resource

4880 Lower Valley Road, Atglen, PA 19310

Steven M. Richman

MW00574550

Other Schiffer Books by Steven M. Richman
Mannequins, 0-7643-2351-2, $49.95

Other Schiffer Books on Related Subjects
Birds of Cape Cod & The Islands, 0-7643-2461-6, $45.00
Jersey City: A Monumental History, 978-0-7643-2638-7,
$24.95

Schiffer Books are available at special discounts for bulk purchases for sales promotions or premiums. Special editions, including personalized covers, corporate imprints, and excerpts can be created in large quantities for special needs. For more information contact the publisher:

Published by Schiffer Publishing Ltd.
4880 Lower Valley Road
Atglen, PA 19310
Phone: (610) 593-1777; Fax: (610) 593-2002
E-mail: Info@schifferbooks.com

For the largest selection of fine reference books on this and related subjects, please visit our
web site at **www.schifferbooks.com**
We are always looking for people to write books on new and related subjects. If you have an
idea for a book please contact us at the above address.

This book may be purchased from the publisher.
Include $3.95 for shipping.
Please try your bookstore first.
You may write for a free catalog.

In Europe, Schiffer books are distributed by
Bushwood Books
6 Marksbury Ave.
Kew Gardens
Surrey TW9 4JF England
Phone: 44 (0) 20 8392-8585; Fax: 44 (0) 20 8392-9876
E-mail: info@bushwoodbooks.co.uk
Website: www.bushwoodbooks.co.uk
Free postage in the U.K., Europe; air mail at cost.

Designed by RoS
Type set in Humansta521 BT

ISBN: 978-0-7643-2822-0
Printed in China

Dedication

To Lucie and Kim.

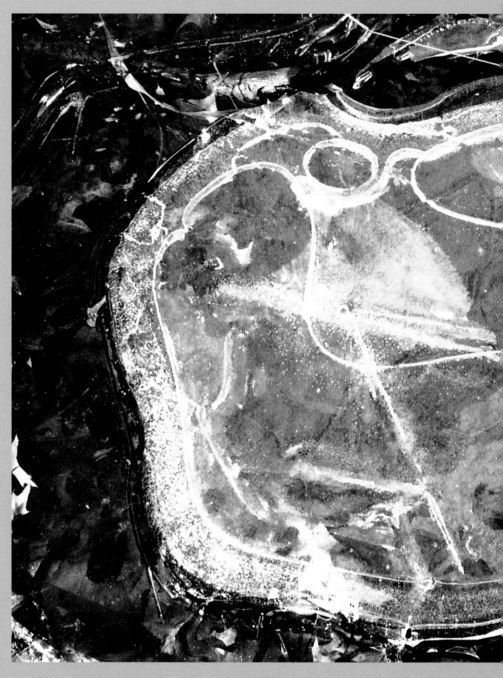

Acknowledgements

This book was made possible through the consistent faith of my editor, Tina Skinner, whose encouragement and frank criticism separated the wheat from the chaff. Thanks also to Jennifer Marie Savage of Schiffer Publishing. Various colleagues have also offered support, and one in particular, Marie Rose Bloomer, has been unflagging in her encouragement and excitement over my projects. I also want to thank Stuart Lederman for introducing me to the Great Swamp Watershed Association.

The Friends of the Great Swamp deserve special credit, as do the Morris County and Somerset County Park Commissions and their staff, for their prodigious efforts in maintaining this phenomenal natural area.

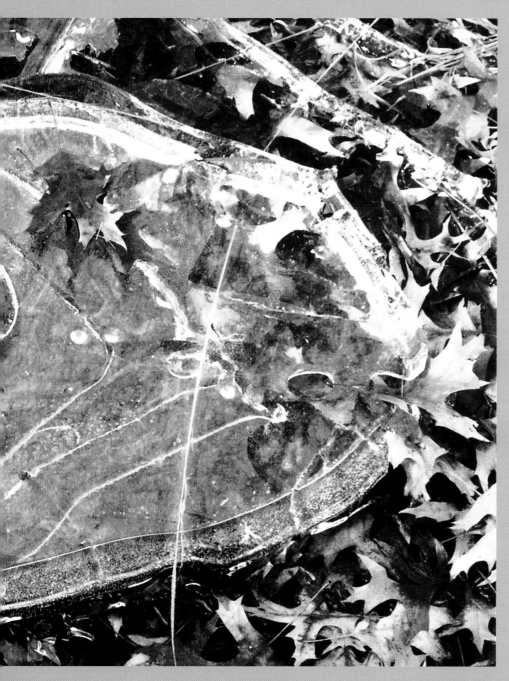

Contents

When I would recreate myself, I seek the darkest wood, the thickest
and most interminable and, to the citizen, most dismal, swamp. I enter
a swamp as a sacred place, a sanctum sanctorum. There is the strength,
the marrow, of Nature. — *Henry David Thoreau, in "Walking"*

Welcome to the Great Swamp.

Introduction

The Great Swamp of New Jersey is a natural area of approximately 7,500 acres that came to be as a result of the Wisconsin Glacier. It is fed by the Passaic River, whose headwaters flow through the nearby Scherman-Hoffman Wildlife Sanctuary that is also part of the area's floodplain. Located just off Interstate Route 287 in the north-central part of New Jersey, the Great Swamp consists generally of four specific areas: 1. Lord Stirling Park; 2. Morris County Great Swamp; 3. Wilderness Area; and 4. Management Area. Separate government and non-profit organizations are responsible for the Great Swamp's management and maintenance as the distinctive place it is.

The Somerset County Park Commission is one of the key players, operating the 950-acre Lord Stirling Park. The northern part of this area contains stables for horseback riding while the southern portion consists of approximately eight and a half miles of trails for relatively easy hiking. Included in that are about three miles of boardwalks. After sustained rain or snowfall, some portions of the trail require appropriate footwear to navigate the saturated ground. The Education Center has a gift shop and bookstore, plus classroom space, as it hosts a variety of activities and classes relating to the Swamp. In the winter, cross-country skiing is permitted on the trails.

Adjacent to Lord Stirling Park to the east is the Great Swamp National Wildlife Refuge, under the auspices of the United States Fish and Wildlife Service. The Refuge consists of lands that were turned over to the Department of the Interior as part of the National Wildlife Refuge system created in the 1960s. It also is listed as a registered National Natural Landmark, which is equivalent to a historical building status.

In the western, or Management Area, active intervention is permitted to manage the ecology. The focus is on maintaining the ecological status of the Swamp. Consequently, active intervention is employed to preserve the character of this area as it is. Visitors are limited to trails and just under a mile of boardwalk that traverse the heart of the Management Area; the trails and boardwalk lead to three separate birding blinds.

Also in this area is Pleasant Plains Road, which crosses Middle Brook and provides a limited "automobile tour" that includes a favored birding outlook. The Refuge Headquarters is located off Pleasant Plains Road, and in addition to the overlook, the trails in this area lead to the three distinct blinds — the Friends Blind, Garden Club Blind, and Sportsmen Blind.

The Friends of the Great Swamp, an independent, non-profit entity established in 1999, operates an information center and a combined bookstore/gift shop in the heart of the Management Area on Pleasant Plains Road, near the Refuge headquarters. Its volunteer board works with the United States Fish and Wildlife Service to support the mission and goals of the Great Swamp, and offers various group and education-related programs. Its website is www.friendsofgreatswamp.org.

On its own property within this geographic area is the Raptor Trust, a separate non-profit corporation formed in 1982 whose mission is to care for and rehabilitate raptor birds. Also off-site but notable for activities in the area is the Audubon Center at the Scherman-Hoffman Wildlife Sanctuary.

However, another important organization whose purview includes the Great Swamp is the Great Swamp Watershed Association, www.greatswamp.org, organized in 1981 to "preserve and protect" not just the Great Swamp's 7,500 acres, but the 36,000 acres of the Great Swamp watershed, that includes four waterways—Black Brook Great Brook, Loantaka Brook and Primrose Brook—and the Passaic River. It provides a teacher's guide to the Swamp, as well as information and suggested activities for hiking and observation of the Great Swamp. The ten municipalities are involved with this watershed region cooperate in policies affecting it under the Ten Towns Great Swamp Watershed Management Committee (www.tentowns.org).

Continuing eastward is the portion of the Refuge that was the first area designated in 1968 as wilderness under the national Wilderness Act of 1964. Hikers have a choice of approximately eight miles of color-coded trails interspersed with the Black Brook, Loantaka Brook and Great Brook that course through this section. Under the terms of the Wilderness Act, the land is under the protection of the President and Congress, and there can be no permanent roads or other structures. Traces of human activity, such as roads and old house sites, were removed. Orientation kiosks and maps are found at selected points in this area. There is not the active intervention to preserve this area as there is in the Management Area.

The fourth area, to the far east, is part of the Morris County Park system. Its 1.4 miles of trails cross swamp, marsh, and upland forest areas, as well as providing an observation blind and deck of its principal pond. The Commission's Great Swamp Outdoor Education Center was dedicated in 1963 and supports a variety of educational and seasonal activities, including the Maple Sugaring Festival in February.

When I refer generally to the Great Swamp, I refer to the entire area, without regard to any particular political region, unless specified.

Under the tree canopy of the swamp, the atmosphere is thick and lush. The swamp is distinguished by water and hardwood. Here, sunlight struggles to penetrate the forest, glinting off the water.

Visitors to the Great Swamp have a choice of diverse activities. Birding is popular, with several blinds located throughout. The Great Swamp is a premiere destination for teams competing in the annual World Series of Birding held in May, in which teams seek to identify the most species of birds. While hiking and cross-country skiing are permitted, there is no camping, fishing, or boating in the Swamp. There is a *Wildlife Tour Route* published by the Friends of the Great Swamp, but there is no driving or bicycling in the Refuge apart from on the paved roads. Organized walks and lectures occur throughout the year.

This book is simply the beginning of a conversation with the profound and often impenetrable essence of the Great Swamp of New Jersey.

The swamp and forest exist in layers, from the organic soil to the ground cover and shrubs, to the higher tree canopies.

The forest of the swamp seems depthless.

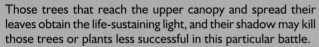

Those trees that reach the upper canopy and spread their leaves obtain the life-sustaining light, and their shadow may kill those trees or plants less successful in this particular battle.

Life is hard for swamp plants, whose roots reach into water or saturated areas; the lack of oxygen causes the leaves to yellow and fall off.

The Swamp is a place of, and for, contemplation and meditation, a place to navigate with open senses.

Dead leaves do not easily decompose, and the decomposition of the leaves of some species may take up to three years.

The autumn light radiates a brilliant red glow.

While a swamp is defined as being wet on at least a semi-permanent but regular basis, the level of water covering different areas changes, based on its various sources, including the overflow from the brooks and rivers and precipitation.

Tussock sedges sprout in the water and fulfill vital ecological functions, including preventing erosion by anchoring the soil and providing refuges for various species.

The still waters reflect almost perfectly, turning the Swamp into two worlds.

Before the snowfall, the cold, wintering Swamp takes on a bluish hue, the verdant greens of summer completely vanished.

Snow brings special challenges to the animals that remain in the Swamp. Ice and snow cover food, and the cold itself can kill.

Winter is also a time of beauty in the Great Swamp as it is reduced to its essence.

The swamp is domi-nated by trees, and the marsh areas by plants in shallow areas.

A submerged, dead leaf; a few drops on another leaf—the beauty of the Swamp is often revealed in its details.

A single leaf escapes from its tree and blows away against a brilliant autumn sky.

Chapter One:

The Establishment of the Swamp

The Airport that Never Was

Politically, the current Great Swamp National Wildlife Refuge was born in turmoil beginning with the announcement in 1959 of the Port Authority of New York and New Jersey's plan to locate an airport in the area. Two separate groups organized in early 1960 to oppose that plan.

One group, the Jersey Jetport Site Association, started a public relations campaign to fight it on political and legal grounds. Those efforts included intense lobbying of the New Jersey Legislature, since the proposed site was just beyond the Port Authority's geographical limits, and approval of both New York and New Jersey would have been needed for the project. Although the New Jersey Legislature passed a bill opposing the expansion, then-governor Robert Meyner vetoed it in 1961. In the next legislative session, the same bill passed again and the new governor, Richard Hughes, signed it.

Paralleling the efforts of the Association during the early 1960s was Marcellus Hartley Dodge, a businessman and philanthropist, who assisted in the acquisition of properties in the area for turnover to the Department of Interior to attempt to remove them from acquisition by the Port Authority. A citizens' group called the Upper Passaic Valley Conservation Committee of Wildlife Preserves was formed into a non-profit corporation that sought to educate the public and raise funds for an education center. This group worked with the National Wildlife Federation and other groups to coordinate acquisition of property by purchase and donation. On May 29, 1964, the Great Swamp Committee of the North American Wildlife Foundation turned over to the United States Department of the Interior 2,600 acres that formed the nucleus of the Refuge. Thereafter, additional acreage was added to grow the Swamp to its current size through the efforts of various entities, including the Great Swamp Conservation Foundation.

The Swamp was also designated a National Natural Landmark in 1966. Designation as such means that the US Secretary of Interior has recognized the Great Swamp as having national significance in terms of its biological and geological components.

A kettle hole was formed by a chunk of ice broken off from the Wisconsin Glacier. This may be one.

The ancient Passaic River reveals its complex personality in different seasons and at different points of its journey through and along the Great Swamp. Here it reflects the fall foliage.

Clouds reflect in the Passaic River in summer.

The Passaic River winds its way towards the great Newark Bay.

A narrow stretch of the Passaic River bordering Lord Stirling Park in the cold of winter.

Different bodies of water exist within the Great Swamp. Streams are moving freshwater that moves from higher levels to lower levels in defined, and usually narrow, channels; brooks and creeks are generally smaller flowing bodies than streams. Lakes are basins fed by freshwater rivers and streams, and are the result of movements of the earth's crust, Ice Age activity, or other activity of the earth since then. The pond is basically a small lake.

20

Trees struggle for life as waters rise and fall, and the fungi facilitate the decomposition and regeneration of the forest.

Along the trails in the Wilderness Area.

A wood duck and Eastern Painted turtles share a platform in the pond in the Morris County Park Commission area of the Great Swamp.

Color coded trail markings on trees reflect the human touch of the governing entities.

This pony truss bridge, carrying Pleasant Plains Road over the Great Brook in the Refuge's Management Area, was built in 1887 by J.P. Bartley & Sons.

Although not within the political boundaries of the Great Swamp, the headwaters of the Passaic River are nonetheless critical to its existence. These scenes show it passing through the Scherman-Hoffman Nature Preserve near the Great Swamp. This is a separate preserve and home to an Audubon Center.

One of the prominent farmers of the Revolutionary era in the area was the Wick family; their house still stands in the nearby Jockey Hollow Encampment, just a few miles from the Great Swamp, where Gen. George Washington kept his troops in 1779-80.

The Great Swamp to the southeast provided part of the strategic protection for Gen. Washington's troops, whose reconstructed huts at the Pennsylvania Brigade encampment site are shown here.

The Maple Sugar Festival in late winter at the Morris County Outdoor Education Center introduces visitors to the tapping of the maple trees, although relatively small amounts of sap are produced.

Chapter Two:

The Nature of the Swamp

The Refuge and the two county parks actually consist of varied types of habitats, not just "swamp." One often hears the terms "swamp," "bog," "fen," and "marsh" used generically and interchangeably to describe "wetlands." When we speak of a swamp, however, we are addressing a natural area that is generally wet with a sizeable percentage of trees. We are concerned here with a non-tidal wetland area; and generally a hardwood swamp common in this part of New Jersey. It is distinguished from a marsh mainly because it is forested with trees and shrubs, whereas an area dominated by plants in shallow water is considered a marsh. A marsh can grow into a swamp as appropriate plants and trees take root there, just as a field can become a forest. Fens and bogs are wetland areas with peat bases; the fen has a mineral-rich peat base, in constrast to the bog. Less than half of the Great Swamp is actually wet, and the slight differences in elevation can be a determination of whether one walks through water or dry land. A swamp "lives" by acquiring silt from the streams, thereby raising the bottom and becoming soil, and ultimately yielding forests.

The Friends of the Great Swamp distribute their own *Guide to Trees and Shrubs*, which identifies twenty-seven trees and shrubs marked along the boardwalk trail in the Management Area. The signature tree of the Great Swamp is the Great Swamp White Oak in the Lord Stirling section. Typical other species in this hardwood swamp include the prevalent red maple and American beech.

The principal river that feeds the Swamp is the Passaic River. This ninety-mile river begins near Mendham, New Jersey, six hundred feet above sea level. It winds its way southward to the outskirts of the Great Swamp, and around Millington, turns northeast past Chatham and Livingston, along the Hatfield Swamp. At Great Piece Meadows, it turns eastward, proceeding to Little Falls and then northeasterly to become part of the Great Falls of Paterson; from there, it flows southward through Dundee Lake and Passaic, where it widens and becomes the much more impressive river spanned in part by the Pulaski Skyway. Ultimately, the river opens into the Newark Bay, where it is joined by its eastern companion, the Hackensack River.

The beginnings of the Swamp are in the Paleozoic Era, 250 million years ago, and the formation of the Appalachian Mountains as a result of the collision of the tectonic plates, or continents now known as Africa and North America. With Africa's separation and departure, molten lava gushed upwards through the surface, resulting in the Watchung Mountains. About forty percent of New Jersey, from Newark through New Brunswick to Trenton and northwest, is the Appalachian Mountain region, including its three components: ridge and valley, highlands, and piedmont. The remaining sixty percent of the state front that line; and to the south and southeast is the coastal plain. The twenty-mile wide piedmont at the foot of the mountains, with elevations of approximately one hundred to three hundred feet, is comprised of crystalline metamorphic and igneous rocks. It is also the setting of the Great Swamp.

The next great age after the Paleozoic is the Mesozoic Era (some 245 to 65 million years ago), the age of volcanoes and dinosaurs, during which the land developed an impermeable base of lava, which hardened over muddy areas—and that formed the impermeable base of the Swamp.

However, it was during the relatively recent Pleistocene Epoch (approximately 1.8 million to 11,000 years ago) of the Cenozoic Era that the last great ice age occurred, and the Great Swamp's origins began. These geologic terms simply divide great periods of time in earth's history; during the Pleistocene Epoch human beings made their appearance, along with many of the species that continue to survive to this day. As temperatures fluctuated, the glaciers melted and retreated. Among the greatest of the glaciers was the Wisconsin Glacier, one of the massive ice sheets that moved southward from the North Pole in a series of advances and retreats over a period lasting from about 100,000 to 10,000 years ago. In colder times, the ice spread southwards; in warmer periods, it melted and the waters retreated northward. Estimates of the times vary, but it appears that by about 12,000 to 16,000 years ago the Wisconsin Glacier was in retreat. The National Park Service notes that the Wisconsin Glacier reached its southernmost point about 25,000 years ago, not only in New Jersey but in Wisconsin as well. As the ice melted, it carried sand and gravel with it that carved out the ground, creating lakes and basins, but over time those lakes dried up — leaving behind swamp and marshland. In the Great Swamp today, "kettles," or surface depressions caused by the melting ice and the collapse of other materials into the ground, are still visible. One presumed kettle in particular is indicated by signage in the eastern Morris County section of the Swamp.

The Wisconsin Glacier at one point dammed the Passaic River with debris as it reached its southernmost point, resulting in the formation of Glacial Lake Passaic, a vast lake that possibly covered a massive area from southern New York, south to the Watchung Mountains, and between the Ramapo Mountains to the west and the Palisades to the east. Various sources put its dimensions at thirty miles long by ten miles wide. It exists today in what we know as the Great Swamp.

The magnitude and variety of life in this place is readily apparent from a few statistics. The Great Swamp is home to some 244 species of birds, six hundred species of plants and trees, (including 215 species of wildflowers), thirty-three species of mammals, twenty-one species of reptiles, eighteen species of amphibians, and twenty-nine species of fish. While containing, perhaps, only a relatively small sampling of the vast amount of species in North America, there are nonetheless certain unique species to the Swamp—such as the Blue-Spotted Salamander, found only in certain counties in New Jersey. The Swamp's Eastern Bluebird breeding population is one of the state's largest. The site is an important stop for migratory birds along the Atlantic Flyway, reinforcing that the Great Swamp's renown for birding activity.

Human Beings In and Around the Swamp

New Jersey's primary aboriginal people were the Lenni Lenape, although the state is reported to have had relatively few Native Americans. "Paleo-Indian hunters" are posited as having been in the Great Swamp area around 12,500 years ago. When European settlers arrived in the area, they found evidence of at least two permanent Lenni Lenape communities near the Great Swamp, and a number of Native American camp sites have been identified in proximity to the Great Swamp. The Great Swamp had provided the agricultural products for their survival as well as animal skins for clothing and trees for canoe transportation. Herbs provided medicinal uses. During the first part of the seventeenth century, the Native Americans were left alone in the area. The Minisink Trail, a significant "Indian trail" in the area and used extensively by the Lenni Lenape, crossed the Swamp's neighboring town of Chatham.

By 1664, the territory that would become New Jersey was divided into East Jersey and West Jersey; certain land in and around the Great Swamp area was obtained at one point by Sir William Penn and his sons. However, it appears that "clear" title passed in 1708, through the "New Britain Purchase," to another group of English investors who acquired the land that included the Great Swamp. It is reported that the Native Americans thought they were granting hunting and fishing rights, but in accordance with non-indigenous law, they lost the land. The area was seen as an impediment to the nascent transportation network linking colonial New York to Philadelphia.

Although these purchases are noted in the early years of the eighteenth century, the various histories of the surrounding towns seem to indicate actual European settlements beginning between 1710 and 1730. Towns like Madison and Chatham, which would have been at the bottom of Lake Passaic, exist now on the end moraines, or deposits of debris, from the Wisconsin Glacier. Farms and mills were the principal occupations as towns developed around the Swamp, and the population remained light. Through the early eighteenth century, the Great Swamp was still wilderness, frequented essentially by hunters and loggers. It was a mixed community; for example, Meyersville, at the southern end of Long Hill Road that divides the Management and Wilderness areas of the Refuge, was named for the German immigrant farmer Kaspar Meyer. Lord Stirling, a general in the Continental army (actually named William Alexander, born in New York) lived in Basking Ridge; the western end of the Great Swamp is named for him.

As the century wore on, many of the farmers in outlying areas nonetheless owned wood lots in the Swamp for providing fuel. A devastating fire in the Great Swamp in 1782, following a period of dryness, burned for weeks, to the detriment of those dependent upon the Swamp's resources. During the Revolution, General George Washington used the Swamp strategically for protection and buffering on one side, and the Watchung Mountains on the other, during his stay in nearby Jockey Hollow. Efforts to farm the land in the nineteenth century were difficult, and despite early twentieth century efforts to drain the area, it remained primarily wetland. By the mid-twentieth century, the communities surrounding the area were less farming than professional, but still had some of the "small town" atmosphere. When the plans for the jetport hit in 1959, the depth of feeling for this place became apparent.

Reportedly, some 250,000 people visit the Great Swamp each year. Photography contests by some of the organizations identified previously reveal a myriad of interpretations. In her book *Stirring the Mud*, Barbara Hurd considers the unique nature of the swamp and writes: "To love a swamp, however, is to love what is muted and marginal, what exists in the shadows, what shoulders its way out of mud and scurries along the damp edges of what is most commonly praised."

What follows is simply the beginning of an interpretation of this special place.

The Lenape Meadow in Lord Stirling Park is preserved as a meadow by annual burning to prevent bushes and trees from crowding out the land. When that is not done, maples and oaks can crowd out the lower vegetation's light, and the area will turn back to forest. This is called succession.

An example of succession is the area known as Woodcock Meadow.

One definition of a swamp is demonstrated in this image of a regularly soggy or wet area with more than half of its area marked by trees.

Woodpecker Swamp in the Lord Stirling area also shows the features of the typical swamp.

The East Marsh along the Red Trail in Lord Stirling Park shows its distinction from swamp areas by its lack of trees.

Varied wetlands exist throughout various areas of the Great Swamp.

This view from the overlook on Pleasant Plains Road shows the interplay of pond, brush, field, and woods.

Along the Orange Trail in an upland section in the Wilderness Area.

The brooks of the Great Swamp are an integral part of the watershed, and feed the Passaic River.

An impenetrable marsh.

The eastern forest, dominated by maples and oaks, turns red, yellow, and orange in the fall.

A turkey vulture, gliding on thermal currents, forms a haunting image framed by the bare branches of trees in winter.

Fallen leaves and watermeal combine to form an abstract painting in the waters of the Great Swamp.

Marsh areas support a variety of vegetation, including a variety of the common spatterdock or yellow pond lily.

The patterns and tracks of the Swamp reflect the presence of often unseen creatures moving through the temporarily drained areas.

Chapter Three:

The Forest

Among the habitats other than "swamp" are dry upland areas, sometimes barely a few feet higher than the wet areas. Unlike political boundaries, the type and mix of trees in the Great Swamp form a borderless community.

In summer, the trees make a rustling sound as the wind pushes through the leaves, and the leaves interact with each other. In winter, the denuded tree branches rub against each other, as neighboring trees' branches sway in the wind and make a haunting, creaking, croaking sound. In the dead of a snowless winter, in the Great Swamp, one can hear the trees conversing as their branches move.

The age of a forest can also be determined by comparable factors such as the kind of canopy overhead, how much space there is between trees, and what kinds of trees are growing. The lower canopied forests with wider spaces reflect younger ones, since those trees are not yet overshadowed by the larger trees, with a higher, tighter canopy that blocks the sun and makes survival more difficult. As portions of the Great Swamp age, the relics of human cultivation retreat.

The tree is in a perpetual battle for survival, seeing to expand its roots and girth to gather energy sufficient to support its growth. Ultimately, whether from the attacks of insects or other creatures, or natural forces such as lightning, or other parasites, the tree dies. the forests of the Great Swamp are simultaneously birthing room and morgue.

The Great Swamp White Oak, a powerful tree and symbol of the forest.

Ranging in size from fifty to ninety feet, it is found along the Red Trail in Lord Stirling Park, near Woodpecker Swamp, shown below in the different seasons.

One can estimate the age of a forest by comparable factors such as the kind of canopy overhead, how much space there is between trees, and what kinds of trees are growing. The lower canopied forests with wider spaces reflect younger ones, since those trees are not yet overshadowed by the larger trees, with a higher, tighter canopy that blocks the sun and makes survival more difficult.

Ultimately, whether from the attacks of insects or other creatures, or natural forces such as lightning, or other parasites, the tree dies. Large, venerable trees lie on the ground...the victim of storm, age, or perhaps humans. They will decompose, feeding insects and fungus among others, and then form part of the forest floor.

The U.S. Fish and Wildlife Service reports that the forests of the Great Swamp range from mature growth to young brush. Mature forests are marked by a thick layer of litter on the floor, as well as fallen and decomposing trees.

The upland regions border different areas, such as marshes and fields.

In the forest, a shagbark hickory (left) battles for light above the forest canopy.

Ferns carpet the forest floor. They are seedless vascular plants that reproduce by spores. Ferns date back to the Devonian Period, approximately 410 to 354 million years ago, and are distinguished by a rhizome, which is an underground stem that supports leaves and roots.

The bark of a tree can become as unique to the individual tree as a fingerprint to a person. While a tree species' bark may have certain biological givens, the color and tone of the bark can be affected by factors that include the soil and age of the tree.

Beech trees provide food for the chipmunks and squirrels of the Swamp forests. The American Beech is well-suited to the swampy area, thriving in areas of surface moisture. Its soft bark also provides an invitation for a segment of another invasive species that delights in disfiguring it.

Maple trees are tapped in winter in the Morris County section.

Vines are climbing plants that compete with trees for survival.

An evergreen tree provides a muted splash of color in the drabness of this winter setting in the Lord Stirling area.

Acorns, the nut of the oak tree, serve not only reproductive purposes for the species, but also provide a significant food source for other animals. Due to their weight, they are not dispersed by the wind, and depend upon animals to carry them appropriate distances from the parent tree in order for them to obtain sufficient room for roots and light.

Various species of birch trees are found in the Great Swamp.

As the wind blows the branches in the canopy, an eerie creaking sound is heard in the winter forest.

Hardwood and evergreen trees seem to greet each other over a path in the Management Section.

This Yellow Birch is one of the "marked" trees to help identify species for the visitor in the *Great Swamp's Guide to Trees and Shrubs*, usually available at the information kiosks.

Shown is black knot fungus in the Scherman-Hoffman Wildlife Sanctuary, which is part of the uplands along the Passaic River that feeds the Great Swamp.

In this scene from the Scherman-Hoffman Wildlife Sanctuary, the ruthless competition of trees reaching upwards towards the light for survival is vividly demonstrated.

A plaque nearby this paper birch, or white birch, in the Lord Stirling section, states that "Indians used the bark from this tree to make their lightweight birchbark canoes. It is recognized by its chalky to creamy white smooth, thin bark with long horizontal lines. It can grow up to 70 feet tall; its wood used for ice cream sticks, bobbins, clothespins, spools, broom handles and toys, as well as pulpwood."

Chapter Four:

Seasons

Seasons are the result of the 23.5 degree tilt of the earth's axis and its elliptical orbit around the sun. The earth is farthest from the sun in the middle of summer in the Northern Hemisphere. However, this hemisphere has more land, which cools and heats faster than water, so that the position of the earth's tilt towards the sun at that time causes the hemisphere to be hotter. Seasons are therefore the result of exposure to the sun, rather than the distance from the sun. That seasons may, in essence, "lag" behind their official times is a function of the storage of heat by the earth and particularly, its oceans. We mark our seasons astronomically, based on the solstices (when the earth's axis tilts most and least towards the sun) and the equinoxes, when the sun is directly over the equator.

The gentleness of the temperature in spring and the emergence of creatures from a myriad of other forms changes the complexion of the Great Swamp. Summer is ruled by the insects and in particular, it seems, the dragonflies. Summer is also the time of the broad vista, the brilliant, endless blue sky and the clouds that remind us of the limited nature of our own atmosphere, and the infinity beyond. With fall, we brace ourselves for the coming winter and the knowledge of things dying. We marvel at the change of color of the foliage, a result of the tree's need to conserve energy during the winter and the cessation of photosynthesis. The act of turning carbon dioxide into oxygen through photosynthesis requires energy. We watch the Great Swamp transform into a palette of color. Finally, in winter, the thick, lush vegetation is stripped bare. Trees are skeletal, silhouetted against the bright blue sky. In a relatively snowless winter, as is becoming more common in New Jersey, the Swamp appears muted, a dullish brown-gray. There is a sharpness now to the Swamp. The cold itself becomes a tangible feature, a reminder of the unforgiving nature of things. With snow, however, the Swamp transforms into another world.

As one walks along the forest paths in spring, signs of new life emerging appear.

Tussock sedge in the swamp and marsh areas show green in spring.

In the waters along the boardwalk in the Management Area, frothy, bubbly masses may be frogs eggs and can be observed in spring.

Throughout the forests of the Swamp, trees begin to flower in the spring. This is a view in the Management Area along one of the boardwalk trails.

A turtle takes advantage of the spring sun to bask.

Another sign of the emergence of spring is the appearance of wildflowers; this one seen in the Management Area.

Summer is marked by the lush green vegetation of the swamp...

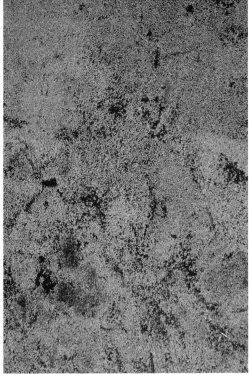

...and the remnants of the fallen leaves of fall and winter on the floor of the mature forest.

The changing colors of the foliage irrefutably announces that fall has arrived in the Swamp.

Fall is also a time of bird migration. New Jersey hosts two species of Canada geese, one that migrates and the other that remains year round, according to the New Jersey Division of Fish, Game and Wildlife.

Gray squirrels nest in trees, which are visible in the winter. This could be one in the Management Area.

Winter is also a time to notice the galls that mutilate trees, as shown here; they're caused by insects, which use them for shelter and nourishment during development.

The snow-encased paths of the Wilderness Area in winter provide a challenge to the hiker, but also provides their own special insight into the Swamp.

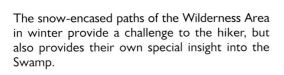

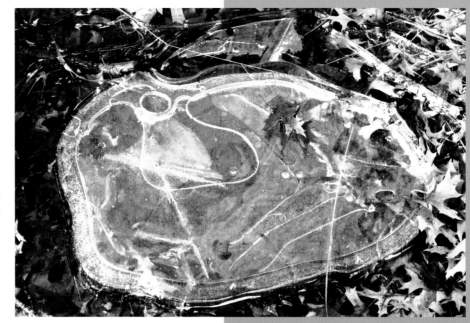

A small puddle of frozen water reveals an abstract painting in the midst of the forest.

A decomposing log, some scattered gumballs from the sweetgum tree, and dead leaves encased in ice and frost reflect the melancholy beauty of winter in the Swamp.

Another sign of winter is the struggle for food; here, a gray squirrel shares the platform of the bird feeder at Sportsmen's Blind with a blue jay.

Chapter Five:

Mushrooms & Fungi

A great diversity of mushrooms and fungi form a vital function in the life cycle of the Great Swamp. Part of the essence of the ecological system, they facilitate the decay that in turn provides nutrients for the trees and plants that themselves sustain other life in the Swamp. Mushrooms absorb nutrients by secreting enzymes to decompose the matter on which they situate themselves. Different types of fungi attach to either dead or living matter. Within their own biological kingdom, they're equal to animals and plants. Unlike plants, which rely on chlorophyll to survive, mushrooms are heterotrophic, meaning they acquire energy by secreting digestive enzymes that break down and absorb organic molecules.

Prevalent in the Swamp are lichens, organisms comprised of two organisms, a fungal and algal component, a symbiosis. The fungus takes in water and minerals (including nitrogen) from air and rain and, since it has no chlorophyll, cannot photosynthesize those nutrients into carbohydrates that are also eventually recycled back into the earth. That is the job of the alga, which is generally either green algae or cyanobacteria (blue-green alga). The job of the fungus also includes shelter; the thallus (its body), which encases the algae, can take one of three forms: foliose (leaflike), crustose (crust-like), and fruticose (indistinct and rounded). The fungus also generally provides the name for the lichen. As a result of their sensitivity to environmental conditions, lichens have become the canary in the mine for concerned naturalists.

I have deliberately avoided specific identification of particular mushrooms for two reasons. First, this book is not intended as a field guide to mushrooms and should not be used as such. Second, my interest was primarily to highlight their role in the aesthetics and ecology of the Great Swamp.

There are a variety of mushrooms and fungi to be found in the Great Swamp, found on trees and growing from the forest floor.

Part of the essence of the ecological system, they facilitate the decay that in turn provides nutrients for the trees and plants that themselves sustain other life in the Swamp.

Mushrooms absorb nutrients by secreting enzymes to decompose the matter on which they situate themselves.

Shelflike mushrooms grow on wood and generally lack stalks.

Mushrooms come in a variety of colors.

Unlike plants, which rely on chlorophyll to survive, mushrooms are heterotrophic, meaning they acquire energy by secreting digestive enzymes that break down and absorb organic molecules.

Sex does not appear to have its enjoyable aspects for mushrooms; they reproduce by releasing their spores into the air.

Shelf mushrooms are well-named. They are prevalent in all areas of the Great Swamp.

52

Mushrooms, like insects, have an outer "skin" composed of chitin, a hard covering, as opposed to the cellulose of plants. Their symmetry can be remarkable.

The origins of mushrooms have been traced to 400 million years ago, probably beginning as singular cell eukaryotes (organisms whose cells possess a nucleus). Contrasting with other plants that are multicellular, fungi are composed of intertwined hyphae (filaments made of individual cells).

Lichens are an organism comprised of two organisms, a fungal and algal component, a symbiosis, but it is not always clear whether that relationship transcends mutual need and becomes merely parasitic. The fungus takes in water and minerals (including nitrogen) from air and rain and, since it has no chlorophyll, cannot photosynthesize those nutrients into carbohydrates that are also eventually recycled back into the earth. That is the job of the alga, which is generally either green algae or cyanobacteria (blue-green alga). The job of the fungus also includes shelter; the thallus (its body), which encases the algae, can take one of three forms: foliose (leaflike), crustose (crust-like), and fruticose (indistinct and rounded).

Capped, stalked mushrooms grow from the forest floor.

Chapter Six:

Reptiles & Amphibians

Reptiles are scaled vertebrates (with the scales, as in the case of turtles, evolving into shell). Amphibians are also vertebrates, but unscaled, and undergo two life phases—larval and adult. Three principal orders comprise amphibians: frogs and salamanders, which are represented in the Great Swamp, and caecilians, wormlike burrowing creatures that are found in tropical areas but not in the Great Swamp. Of the four orders of reptiles, (1) turtles and tortoises and (2) lizards and snakes are represented in the Great Swamp; (3) alligators and crocodiles, and (4) tuataras are not.

Because both amphibians and reptiles are "ectothermal" in that their body temperature depends upon the external environment, although amphibians lack the scales that distinguish reptiles, a necessary behavior is basking. This allows the body temperature to be warmed by the outside heat. Not all ectothermal creatures are actually "cold blooded" in a literal sense since some may have temperatures warmer than humans. Throughout the Great Swamp, in season, we can observe this activity.

The Northern Water Snake is common in the Great Swamp, and is marked by regular bands. They are not poisonous, but can attack fiercely and emit an anticoagulant, thereby causing profuse bleeding.

In spring, the Water Snake emerges from hibernation.

The American Snapping Turtle is found in the Great Swamp. Snappers can reach weights of forty-five pounds in the wild, and spend considerable time in the water, often burying themselves in the mud with only eyes and nostrils exposed. This one was pictured in the Management Section just before vanishing from sight.

Above: The Spotted Turtle hibernates in winter. Come summer, this turtle will spend its time underground. While it may be seen with some facility in the spring, when it also basks, it is not so easy to locate in summer and fall.
Below: This painted turtle seems ready to fly.

The Eastern Painted Turtle, one of the most common of North American turtles, is shown here covered in watermeal.

Painted turtles bask together when they cannot find sufficient space to bask alone.

Basking not only allows the turtle to regulate its body temperature, but also enables it to shed itself of parasites and possibly absorb vitamins through ultraviolet rays.

It is not uncommon to see turtles basking head to tail, particularly when available space is limited.

Here, four turtles crowd to bask in the bright sun.

The Eastern painted turtle generally swims and feeds near the surface of the water.

There are five different species of Leopard frogs in North America. They vary in spot patterns and color. The most common in New Jersey would be the Northern and Southern Leopard Frogs. The Relict Leopard Frog and Rio Grande Leopard Frog are found in the southwestern United States. The Plains Leopard Frog is found in the central part of the country. According to the *Audubon Guide to North American Reptiles and Amphibians*, a sixth variety, the Las Vegas Leopard Frog, was last seen in 1942 and is probably extinct; its range was limited to Clark County, Nevada,

Green Frogs may also be tan or brown, and the male's voice sounds like a banjo being strummed. Often confused with bullfrogs, they may be distinguished by the pronounced dorsal lateral ridge, as shown here, that starts from behind the eyes. Interestingly, it is not uncommon to find them as this one, with a green head and olive-brown body, according to the Cleveland Museum of Natural History website.

Bullfrogs live at least five or six years, and can be varied in color, including even albino or blue, but generally, green brown or tan.

This bullfrog was observed in late May. The off-white throat color is typical of a female; the males have yellow throats.

Chapter Seven:

Birds

Contemporary thinking now holds that birds are not merely descended from dinosaurs, but actually are dinosaurs, at least in an evolved form. The non-avian dinosaurs that are extinct are just that; it is therefore acceptable, at least to certain portions of the scientific community, to refer to present-day birds as "avian dinosaurs." So again, with a bit of imagination, we can transport ourselves to not merely another age, but to a completely new way of thinking and seeing the world around us, through this microcosm of the Swamp. Birds are an inseparable and integral part of the life and essence of the Great Swamp. They are the often heard and unseen owners of the forest.

Perhaps the Swamp's signature bird is the Eastern Bluebird, common through all four seasons. Throughout the Swamp are the birdhouses built for it. Houses like this are often set out in "bluebird trails" to facilitate the species.

Equally interesting to observe are the observers themselves, the birders who carry on their own conversations with the Great Swamp and area as much a part of it as their avian counterparts.

The Great Egret, of the Heron family, is occasionally seen in the Great Swamp in spring, summer and fall, but rarely in winter.

The Great Egret feeds in both water, as seen here, on amphibians and small fish, and also on land, where it eats small animals and insects.

The graceful Great Egret in flight.

Mute swans, not native to North America, nonetheless form a common part of the landscape.

Another impressive member of the Heron family, the Great Blue Heron, is more commonly observed in the Great Swamp. It eats fish, as well as frogs, crayfish, and various insects, and sounds more like frog than a bird.

Among the Swamp's signature birds is the Eastern Bluebird, common in the Great Swamp through all four seasons. It nests in tree cavities, old woodpecker holes, and bird boxes like those in the Swamp, from three to twenty feet above ground, and in holes in tree stumps.

The Swamp Sparrow is common to the Great Swamp; this one contemplates its surroundings in the Management Area.

A hummingbird flaps its wings on average of fifty times per second, in the motion of a figure "8."

Red-Tailed Hawk, glimpsed here in the Morris County Park section.

A splash of yellow in the barren forest as this bird hops from one branch to another, caught in motion.

The Blue Jay is reported to be among the most intelligent of birds, and is observed here from Sportsmen Blind.

The Tufted Titmouse is a frequent visitor to this feeder in the Management Area in winter.

The Nuthatch is particularly agile.

Black-Capped Chickadee eating.

The American Robin is the largest North American member of the Thrush family, seen here basking in the sun at the bird overlook on Pleasant Plains Road in the Management Area. Its wings are spread to gather warmth.

The Gray Catbird, a member of the Mockingbird family, like the American Robin, is abundant at all times of the year except winter.

Tree Swallows are common birds, abundant in the Great Swamp in all seasons except winter, which it spends in the Southern United States or in Central America.

The Mallard is very common duck, and is easily recognized by its brilliant coloring in the male, and the brown-mottled female. They are often seen in male-female pairs, or groups of pairs, and are generally monogamous.

The Red-winged Blackbird is also abundant through all but the winter season; its habitat, in addition to freshwater marshes, includes open fields and pastures.

The Downy Woodpecker is common in the Great Swamp through all four seasons, and is the smallest of North American woodpeckers.

The Red-Bellied Woodpecker is a seed-eater and often seen at feeders.

A Cardinal and a Blue Jay share a tree. The Blue Jay is reported to be among the most intelligent of birds.

A flock of birds in winter seems almost Hitchcockian.

The Mourning Dove

A dragonfly devouring its prey.

Chapter Eight:

Insects

It is not known, precisely, how many species of insects exist, but it is accepted that we do not know all the species. There are presently over 900,000 known species, and just over ten percent of that number are known in the United States. The Smithsonian Institute reports that at any given time, there are 10 quintillion (10,000,000,000,000,000,000) individual insects alive. Forty-one states have official "state insects;" New Jersey shares the honey bee with Arkansas, Georgia, Kansas, Louisiana, Maine, Mississippi, Missouri, Nebraska, North Carolina, Oklahoma, South Dakota, Tennessee, Utah, Vermont and Wisconsin. What insects may lack in individual intelligence they make up for in perseverance and endurance. They survive.

A dragonfly will "obelisk" and extend its abdomen in this fashion to reduce exposure to the sun.

Dragonfly species exhibit different levels of territoriality. Among those males to obtain territory, the behavior varies considerably. Some protect territory for limited periods during the day, and while they are out of the territory, others of the species may protect the territory while they are in it—a kind of time-sharing arrangement. Still others protect several territories, patrolling each for limited periods throughout the day.

A dragonfly lands on a leaf. He is soon chased away by the apparent owner of the territory. Another may come and suffers the same fate. They form an intricately choreographed dance of settle and chase. To the human eye, the territory is abstract, yet the three-dimensional boundaries of it seem clearly known to the dragonfly.

The Twelve-Spotted Skimmer is one of the more commonly seen dragonflies in the Great Swamp, and is found throughout the United States.

This Meadowhawk dragonfly seems to be basking.

A Spangled Skimmer perches horizontally on water lilies.

This Blue Dauber is at rest with wings forward.

Mating dragonflies in the "wheel" position in the Management Area in late May.

Caterpillars are the larval stage of butterflies. This one seemed to form a question mark in silhouette, seen from beneath the leaf—another example of the surprises that the details of the Swamp hold for the alert viewer.

Because of its limited memory capacity, the individual cabbage white will generally pursue nectar, its main food source, from the same type of flowers so that it does not have to learn how to retrieve it from too many different types. It basks with its wings towards the sun to reflect the warmth towards the darker parts of its body. One spot means male; two spots are the females.

Pearly Crescentspot butterflies are described by the Audubon guide as "highly pugnacious."

Clouded Skipper butterflies are common to the lowland fields and grasslands of the Great Swamp.

The Little Wood Satyr butterfly is one of about fifty species of satyrs in North America, and remarkable for its long flight periods.

The Monarch butterfly is famous for its species' north-south annual migrations.

There are approximately 250 species of Skippers in North America.

A crane fly pauses on the trail, and then seems to flutter quickly up and down. She stops. Closer inspection reveals her ovipositor in the ground, and she is steady as she lays her eggs.

A butterfly and beetle share a flower.

The common housefly in the "wild."

One common species to the Great Swamp is the carpenter ant, which takes its name from its penchant for carving out its colonies in wood.

Bees are among the most socialized of insects, with the hive hierarchy consisting of the queen, a few male drones, and the female worker bees. Bees are also among the most aerodynamically unsound creatures, and when they wear their wings out, and can no longer be of use, they die alone.

The wasp conjures up a different image, that of the lone, focused killer hunter. Although they share an insect order with ants and bees, many species are not social in the sense of inhabiting colonies, or at least not on the vast scale of ants and bees. As parasites, they also play a vital role in the ecological balance of the Swamp, maintaining population levels of other insects, and serving as food for other species themselves.

The Japanese Beetle is not native to North America and, inadvertently introduced in 1916, became a major and destructive presence on the continent.

Spittlebug nymphs are found within this mixture as protection from predators. This was found in the Lenape Meadow in the Lord Stirling Park section.

Chapter Nine:

Wildflowers

Wildflowers are the splashes of color in the palette of this place. Particularly in the summer, they provide relief from the overwhelming greenness of the Great Swamp. Providing a carpet on the forest floor are the ferns. Ferns are seedless vascular plants that reproduce by spores, and date back to the Devonian Period, approximately 410 to 354 million years ago, when insects and spiders also appeared. Over thirty years ago, two botanists from Drew University, Robert and Florence Zuck, were cataloguing the Great Swamp's plant life. As reported by Thomas in his book *The Swamp*, at that time they believed "there may be as many as a thousand species ... Among them are twenty-three types of moss, sixteen ferns, seven kinds of goldenrod, nine different asters, and a large number of grasses and sedges. It is...a botanical paradise of great scientific and aesthetic value."

Wildflowers are the splashes of color in the palette. Particularly in the summer, they provide relief from the overwhelming greenness of the Swamp.

Over thirty years ago, two botanists from Drew University, Robert and Florence Zuck, were cataloguing the Great Swamp's plant life and at that time believed "there may be as many as a thousand species ... Among them are twenty-three types of moss, sixteen ferns, seven kinds of goldenrod, nine different asters, and a large number of grasses and sedges. It is ... a botanical paradise of great scientific and aesthetic value." (Thomas, 26).

Grasses of the Swamp.

The cattail is a source of food and medicine for humans as well as forming an integral part of the ecology of wetlands. It turns brown as it begins to pollinate, and seems to explode when it releases its seeds.

Thistle

Holly

Swamp Rose Mallow

Black-Eyed Susan

Tickseed Sunflower

Ox-Eye Daisy

Purple Loosestrife

Swamp Honeysuckle

Yarrow with weevils

Marsh fern

Swamp Milkweed

Common Milkweed pod

Chicory

Button Bush

Chapter Ten:

Mammals

Approximately thirty species of mammals inhabit the Great Swamp, including various types of tree-living squirrels—the common Eastern Gray, the Red, and the Southern Flying. The Eastern Gray Squirrel is indigenous to North America. There are both arboreal and terrestrial squirrels, but the Eastern Gray, the most commonly seen squirrel in the Great Swamp, is arboreal. Its tail functions as a rudder that assists in climbing and navigating its leaps between trees. They build their nests in trees, including the most common ones in the Great Swamp—the White Oak, American Beech, American Elm, Red Maple, and Sweetgum. In winter, their leafy nests are easy to see. The Eastern Chipmunk is a terrestrial squirrel. Neither the Eastern Gray Squirrel nor the Eastern Chipmunk hibernate as such, but both become relatively inactive in winter.

The Eastern Gray Squirrel is indigenous to North America. There are both arboreal and terrestrial squirrels, but the Eastern Gray, the most commonly seen squirrel in the Great Swamp, is arboreal.

Eastern Chipmunks spend most of their waking time foraging for food, with frequent trips back to the burrow.

Human wreckage: "Plymouth Reck." As mammals in the Great Swamp, human beings have made a unique presence.

The headquarters of the Friends of the Great Swamp, in the Management Area, on Pleasant Plains Road.

This boardwalk provides a way for humans (people) to make their way through parts of The Great Swamp.

The Environmental Education Center at Lord Stirling Park, run by the Somerset County Park Commission, on Lord Stirling Road.

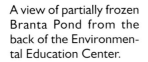

A view of partially frozen Branta Pond from the back of the Environmental Education Center.

This is presumed to be a kettle hole, formed by a chunk of ice broken off from the Wisconsin Glacier, in the Morris County section of the area.

The Great Swamp Outdoor Education Center operated by the Morris County Park Commission.

The West Observation Blind in Lord Stirling Park provides a view of Branta Pond and Bullfrog Pond.

This information kiosk at the main entrance to the Management Area off Long Hill Road provides an orientation to the trails (principally boardwalk) and some of the animal and plant life to be found. Maps and other brochures are available nearby.

The trailhead on Long Hill Road to the Blue Trail in the Wilderness Area helps orient the visitor.

Friends Blind in the Management Area.

Garden Club Blind looks out towards Middle Brook in the Management Area.

Fields and forests, water and sky, blend together in a palette of color.

From the observation deck at the pond along the Orange Loop at the Morris County Park Commission's Great Swamp area, we experience the serene beauty of the Great Swamp.

Conclusion

The Great Swamp is a microcosm of life on earth. It is a place of unceasing struggle, a Hobbesian world where for many of its denizens life is "solitary, poor, nasty, brutish, and short." And yet it is a place of heart-stopping beauty and poignancy, a place where life is reaffirmed as it has been since the Wisconsin Glacier retreated over this area, leaving behind the placenta that nourished this wetland. It is a vast metropolis with many neighborhoods, a place of power and mystery, of intrigue, of silence and noise. It is a place where one may come, in the midst of the most densely populated state in the nation, to find resonance in the strange and familiar.

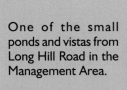

One of the small ponds and vistas from Long Hill Road in the Management Area.

If we look down, we may be surprised by the abstract patterns.

Trails sometimes dry may be saturated after heavy precipitation.

Color coded trails in the Wilderness Area, Stirling Park, and the Morris County section orient the hiker.

An insect's eye view provides a different perspective.

The Great Swamp may occasionally take on a surreal aspect that reminds one of a painting by Yves Tanguy, where strange figures inhabit a seemingly horizonless space.

Nature's Gallery

The Great Swamp is an art museum of abstract expressionism, of surrealism, of still life. When we look at the tangle of vines and branches, perhaps we see the strong lines of a Pollock painting and abstract expressionism. To the extent that type of work relied on freely applied paint on large canvases, the life-size mass of vines and branches reflects this. And when we see the muted colors of leaves and forest floor debris beneath ice, we discern the shadings of a Monet Impressionist painting. With little effort, when we see the eye-like markings on the bark of an American Beech tree, we see a Magritte. We experience nature on a variety of levels, including the "found art" for those who are open to it.

The Great Swamp remains a place of menace and treachery in the struggle for survival.

It could also take on the image of a Jackson Pollock painting, where thick paint forms an intricate abstraction of intertwining lines.

The remains of a crayfish shell make an eerie still life.

Like an artist exploring the reaches of color of the palette, the Great Swamp provides an endless variation...

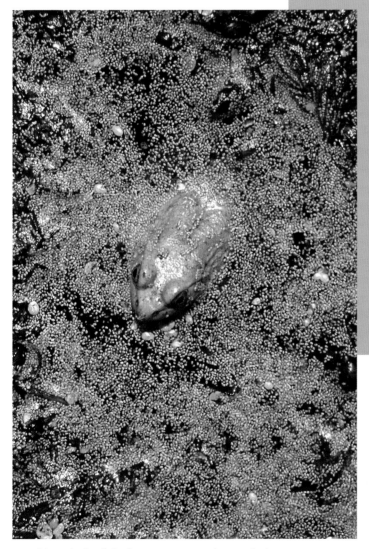

...although the fight for oxygen remains a priority.

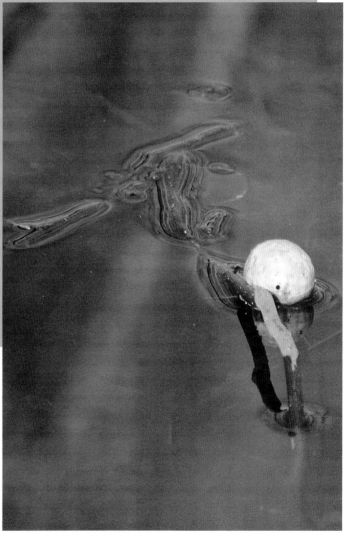

For the artist, the Swamp is a place of shapes, both spherical...

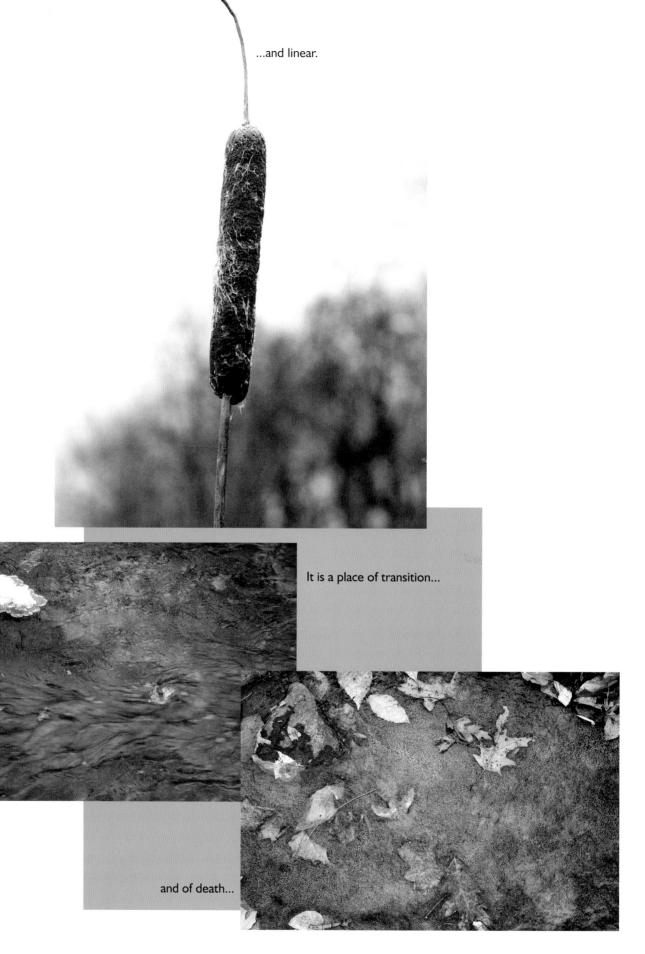

...and linear.

It is a place of transition...

and of death...

...and of strange lives in hard places, but ultimately...

It's a place of balance...

...and wonder.

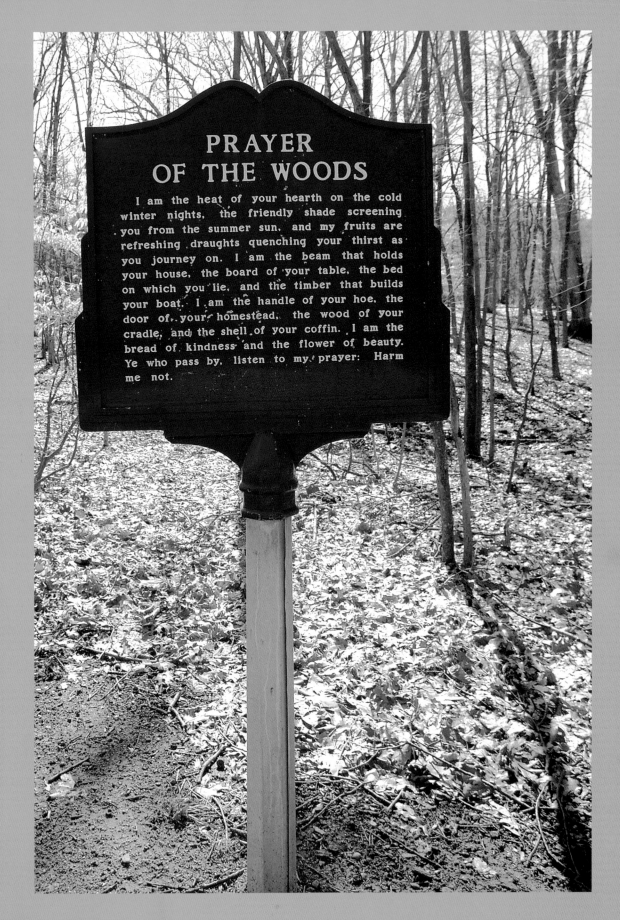

PRAYER OF THE WOODS

I am the heat of your hearth on the cold winter nights, the friendly shade screening you from the summer sun, and my fruits are refreshing draughts quenching your thirst as you journey on. I am the beam that holds your house, the board of your table, the bed on which you lie, and the timber that builds your boat. I am the handle of your hoe, the door of your homestead, the wood of your cradle, and the shell of your coffin. I am the bread of kindness and the flower of beauty. Ye who pass by, listen to my prayer: Harm me not.

The Prayer of the Woods in the Morris County Park Commission portion of the Great Swamp brings us back to the spirit of Thoreau.

Author's Note: The following were consulted in the course of preparing this book and also contains a selected set of recommended reading and field guides for those venturing into the Great Swamp or comparable places.

Adams, Douglas and Mark Carwardine. *Last Chance to See.* New York, New York: Ballantine Books (Random House Publishing Group), 1990.

Alden, Peter and Brian Cassie. *National Audubon Society Field Guide to the Mid-Atlantic States.* New York, New York: Chanticleer Press, Inc. [Alfred A. Knopf, Inc.], 1999.

Allaby, Michael, ed. *Oxford Dictionary of Zoology (2d ed.).* Oxford, England: Oxford University Press, 1999.

Oxford Dictionary of Plant Sciences. Oxford, England: Oxford University Press, 2004.

Ardrey, Robert. *The Territorial Imperative.* New York, New York: Dell Publishing Company, Inc., 1966.

Attenborough, David. *The Life of Birds.* Princeton, New Jersey: Princeton University Press, 1998.

The Living Planet. Boston, Massachusetts and Toronto, Canada: Little, Brown and Company, 1984.

The Trials of Life: A Natural History of Animal Behavior. Boston, Massachusetts and Toronto, Canada: Little, Brown and Company, 1990.

Life on Earth. Boston, Massachusetts and Toronto, Canada: Little, Brown and Company, 1979.

Behler, John L. *The Audubon Society Field Guide to North American Reptiles and Amphibians.* New York, New York: Chanticleer Press, Inc. [Alfred A. Knopf, Inc.], 1979.

Bode, Carl, ed. *The Portable Thoreau.* New York, New York: The Viking Press, 1947, 1975.

Borgioli, A. and G. Cappelli. *The Living Swamp.* London, England: Orbis Publishing Ltd., 1979.

Borror, Donald J. and Richard E. White. *A Field Guide to Insects.* Boston, Massachusetts: Houghton Mifflin Company, 1970.

Brooks, Steve. *Dragonflies.* Washington, D.C.: Smithsonian Books, 2003.

Bull, John and John Farrand, Jr. *The Audubon Society Field Guide to North American Birds, Eastern Edition.* New York, New York: Chanticleer Press, Inc. [Alfred A. Knopf, Inc.], 1977.

Brydon, Norman F. *The Passaic River: Past, Present, Future.* New Brunswick, New Jersey: Rutgers University Press, 1974.

Carrighar, Sally. *One Day at Teton Marsh.* Reprint: Lincoln, Massachusetts and London, England: University of Nebraska Press, 1979.

Carroll, David M. *Swampwalker's Journal: A Wetlands Year.* Boston, Massachusetts and New York, New York: Houghton Mifflin Company, 1999. First Mariner Books Edition, 2001.

Self-Portrait with Turtles. Boston, Massachusetts and New York, New York: Houghton Mifflin Company, 1999. First Mariner Books Edition, 2004.

Cavanaugh, Cam. *Saving the Great Swamp: The People, the Power Brokers, and an Urban Wilderness.* Frenchtown, New Jersey: Columbia Publishing Company, Inc., 1978.

De Santis, Salvatore. "An Introduction to Lichens." http://www.nybg.org/bsci/lichens/. Accessed January 7, 2007.

Duffey, Eric. *The Forest World: The Ecology of the Temperate Woodlands.* New York, New York: A&W Publishers, Inc., 1980.

Eastman, John. *The Book of Swamp and Bog.* Harrisburg, Pennsylvania: Stackpole Books, 1995.

The Book of Forest and Thicket. Harrisburg, Pennsylvania: Stackpole Books, 1992.

Eiseley, Loren. *The Immense Journey.* New York, New York: Vintage Books, Random House, Inc., 1957.

Emerson, Ralph Waldo. *Nature.* 1836. http://oregonstate.edu/instruct/phl302/texts/emerson/nature-contents.html

Finch, Robert. *Common Ground: A Naturalist's Cape Cod.* [David R. Godine, Publisher, Inc., 1981.] New York, New York: W. W. Norton & Company, 1981.

Finch, Robert and John Elder, eds. *The Norton Book of Nature Writing.* New York, New York and London, England: W. W. Norton & Company, 1990.

Frome, Michael. *Battle for the Wilderness.* New York, New York: Praeger Publishers, 1974.

Gardner, T. "Declining Amphibian Populations: A Global Phenomenon in Conservation Biology." *Animal Biodiversity and Conservation.* 2001.

Gibbons, J. Whitfield and Michael E. Dorcas. *North American Watersnakes: A Natural History.* Norman, Oklahoma: University of Oklahoma Press, 2004.

Goin, Coleman J. and Olive B. Goin. *Introduction to Herpetology, 2nd ed.).* San Francisco, California: W. H. Freeman and Company, 1971.

Heinrich, Bernd. *The Trees in My Forest.* New York, New York: Cliff Street Books (HarperCollins imprint), 1997. Ecco ppbck., 2003.

Winter World: The Ingenuity of Animal Survival. New York: Cliff Street Books (HarperCollins imprint), 2003. Ecco ppbck., 2004.

Hurd, Barbara. *Stirring the Mud: On Swamps, Bogs, and Human Imagination.* Boston, Massachusetts: Beacon Press, 2001; Mariner Books, 2003.

Hutchins, Ross E. *Insects.* Englewood Cliff, New Jersey: Prentice Hall, Inc., 1966.

Johnson, George B. and Peter H. Raven. *Biology: Principles and Explorations.* Austin, Texas: Holt, Rinehart and Winston, 2001.

Krautwurst, Terry. "Bark is Beautiful." *Mother Earth News.* February/March 2006, www.motherearthnews.com.

Krebs, Ernst (text) and Heinrich Gohl (photographs). *Living Forests.* London, England: Kaye & Ward Ltd., 1975. New York, New York: Oxford University Press, 1975. Transl. Frederick and Christine Crowley.

Kricher, John C. and Gordon Morrison. *A Field Guide to Ecology of Eastern Forests.* New York, New York: Houghton Mifflin Company, 1988.

Larousse Encyclopedia of Animal Life. New York, London, Toronto, Sidney, Johannesburg: McGraw-Hill Book Company, 1967.

Lawrence, Susannah and Barbara Gross. *The Audubon Society Field Guide to the Natural Places of the United States: Inland.* New York, New York: Pantheon Books, 1984.

Lincoff, Gary H. *National The Audubon Society Field Guide to North American Mushrooms.* New York, New York: Chanticleer Press, Inc. [Alfred A. Knopf, Inc.], 1981.

Little, Elbert L. *National Audubon Society Field Guide to North American Trees (Eastern Region)*. New York, New York: Chanticleer Press, Inc. [Alfred A. Knopf, Inc.], 1980.

Logan, William Bryant. *Oak: The Frame of Civilization*. New York, New York and London, England: W. W. Norton and Co., Inc., 2005.

Long, Kim. *Frogs: A Wildlife Handbook*. Boulder, Colorado: Johnson Printing, 1999.

Longwood, William. *The Queen Must Die and Other Affairs of Bees and Men*. New York, New York and London, England: W. W. Norton and Co., Inc., 1985.

Lopez, Barry. *Field Notes*. New York, New York: Alfred A. Knopf, 1994.

Lorenz, Konrad Z. *King Solomon's Ring*. New York, New York: Harper & Row Publishers, Inc., 1952. First published Methuen & Co., Ltd., 1952. Transl. Marjorie Kerr Wilson. Reprinted 1980, Time-Life Books.

Lorenzi, Rossella. "Found! Turtle from Dinosaur Age." http://www.abc.net.au/science/news/stories/2005/1516133.htm. December 16, 2006.

Lyons, Janet and Sandra Jordan. *Walking the Wetlands*. New York, Chichester, Brisbane, Toronto and Singapore: John Wiley & Sons, Inc., 1989.

McKnight, Kent H. and Vera B. McKnight. *A Field Guide to Mushrooms*. New York, New York and Boston, Massachusetts: Houghton Mifflin Company, 1987.

Milne, Lorus and Margery Milne. *National Audubon Society Field Guide to North American Insects and Spiders (Eastern Region)*. New York, New York: Chanticleer Press, Inc. [Alfred A. Knopf, Inc.], 1996.
Patterns of Survival. Englewood Cliffs, New Jersey: Prentice-Hall, Inc., 1967.

Niering, William A. and Nancy C. Olmstead. *The Audubon Society Field Guide to North American Wildflowers (Eastern Region)*. New York, New York: Chanticleer Press, Inc. [Alfred A. Knopf, Inc.], 1979.

Nikula, Blair and Jackie Sones, Donald Stokes, Lillian Stokes. *Beginner's Guide to Dragonflies*. Boston, New York, London: Little Brown and Company, 2002.

Oldroyd, Harold. *The Natural History of Flies*. New York, New York: W. W. Norton and Co., Inc., [First American Edition] 1965.

Patent, Dorothy Hinshaw and William Muñoz. *Biodiversity*. New York, New York: Clarion Books, Houghton Mifflin Company, 1996.

Peterson, Roger Tory and Margaret McKenny. *A Field Guide to Wildflowers*. Boston, Massachusetts: Houghton Mifflin Company, 1968.

Pettigrrew, Laurie. *New Jersey Wildlife Viewing Guide*. Helena, Montana: Falcon Publishing, Inc., 1998.

Pielou, E.C. *Fresh Water*. Chicago, Illinois and London, England: University of Chicago Press, 1998.

Pyle, Robert Michael. *The Audubon Society Field Guide to North American Butterflies*. New York, New York: Alfred A. Knopf, Inc., 1981.

Quammen, David. *Natural Acts: A Sidelong View of Science and Nature*. New York, New York: Avon Books, 1985.

Rhodes, Dennis. *New Jersey Wildlife Illustrated*. Union City, New Jersey: William H. Wise and Company, Inc., 1977.

Stafford, Peter. *Snakes*. Washington, D.C.: Smithsonian Institution Press, 2000.

Stansfield, Charles A. *A Geography of New Jersey, 2nd Ed*. New Brunswick, New Jersey and London, England: Rutgers University Press, 1983.

Stokes, Donald. *A Guide to Nature in Winter*. Boston, New York, Toronto, London: Little Brown and Company, 1976.

Stokes, Donald and Lillian Stokes. *Stokes Field Guide to Birds, Eastern Region*. Boston, New York, Toronto, London: Little Brown and Co., 1996.
A Guide to Bird Behavior, Vols. I, II and III. Boston, New York, Toronto, London: Little Brown and Co., 1979, 1983, 1989.

Stokes, Donald and Lillian Stokes and Ernest Williams. *The Butterfly Book*. Boston, New York, Toronto, London: Little Brown and Co., 1991.

Suzuki, David and Wayne Grady. *Tree: A Life Story*. Vancouver, Canada: Greystone Books, division of Douglas & McIntyre, Ltd., 2004.

Taylor, T. N. and H. Hass, W. Remy and H. Kerp. "The Oldest Fossil Lichen." http://www.uni-muenster.de/GeoPalaeontologie/Palaeo/Palbot/nature.html. Accessed January 7, 2007.

Terres, John K. *The Audubon Society Encyclopedia of North American Birds*. New York, New York: Random House (Wings Books Division), 1996 [by arrangement with Alred A. Knopf, Inc].

Thayer, Theodore. *Colonial and Revolutionary Morris County*. Morristown, New Jersey: Compton Press, Inc./Morris County Heritage Commission, 1975.

Thomas, Bill. *The Swamp*. New York, New York: W. W. Norton & Company, Inc., 1976.

Thomas, Lewis. *The Medusa and the Snail: More Notes of a Biology Watcher*. New York, New York: The Viking Press, 1979.

Tiner, Ralph W. *In Search of Swampland: A Wetland Sourcebook and Field Guide*. New Brunswick, New Jersey: Rutgers University Press, 1998.
Wetland Indicators: A Guide to Wetland Identification, Delineation, Classification and Mapping. Boca Raton, London, New York, Washington: CRC Press LLC (Lewis Publishers), 1999.

Tudge, Colin. *The Tree*. New York, New York: Crown Publishers, Division of Random House, 2005, 2006.

Tyning, Thomas F. *Stokes Nature Guides: A Guide to Amphibians and Reptiles*. Boston, New York, Toronto, London: Little, Brown and Company, 1990.

Ursin, Michael J. *Life In and Around Freshwater Wetlands*. New York, New York: Thomas Y. Crowell Company, 1975.

USDA Forest Service. *Silvics of North America*. http://www.na.fs.fed.us/pubs/silvics_manual/table_of_contents.shtm. Accessed January 6, 2007.

Vanner, Michael. *The Encyclopedia of North American Birds*. New York, New York: Barnes and Noble Books, 2005.

Wilson, Edward O. *In Search of Nature*. Washington, D.C. and Covelo, California: Shearwater Books (Island Press), 1996.

Yoffe, Emily. "Silence of the Frogs." *New York Times Magazine*. December 13, 1992.

Zimmer, Carl. "Devious Butterflies, Full-Throated Frogs and Other Liars." *The New York Times*. December 26, 2006.